W9-AJO-598

WITHDRAWN

ALL ABOARD AMERICA

Niagara Falls

ABDO
Publishing Company

A Buddy Book
by
Sarah Tieck

VISIT US AT
www.abdopublishing.com

Published by ABDO Publishing Company, 8000 West 78th Street, Edina, Minnesota 55439.

Copyright © 2008 by Abdo Consulting Group, Inc. International copyrights reserved in all countries. No part of this book may be reproduced in any form without written permission from the publisher. Buddy Books™ is a trademark and logo of ABDO Publishing Company. Printed in the United States.

Contributing Editor: Michael P. Goecke
Graphic Design: Deborah Coldiron
Cover Photograph: Photos.com
Interior Photographs/Illustrations: Library of Congress (pages 15, 17); Photos.com (pages 5, 6, 7, 9, 12, 13, 16, 19, 21, 22)

Library of Congress Cataloging-in-Publication Data

Tieck, Sarah, 1976-
    Niagara Falls / Sarah Tieck.
        p. cm. — (All aboard America)
    Includes bibliographical references and index.
    ISBN 978-1-59928-938-0
    1. Niagara Falls (N.Y. and Ont.)—Juvenile literature. I. Title.

F127.N8T54 2008
974.7'99—dc22
                                                    2007027269

Table of Contents

Niagara Falls is a group of waterfalls. The falls are located in eastern North America, where the United States borders Canada.

For hundreds of years, people have visited beautiful Niagara Falls. It is a famous, historic **landmark**.

Niagara Falls is among the largest waterfalls in the world.

Niagara Falls is also an important natural **resource**. The waters have power. This provides electricity to parts of the United States and Canada.

Water from Lake Erie flows into the Niagara River. Then, it falls over cliffs of shale and dolomite rocks.

Niagara Falls is very wide. It includes American, Bridal Veil, and Canadian falls.

American Falls is shaped a bit like a *W*.

Bridal Veil Falls has had other names over the years. At one time it was called Luna Falls. At another, it was known as Iris Falls.

Because of its rounded U shape, Canadian Falls is also known as Horseshoe Falls.

American Falls is near Prospect Point Park. The falls are separated from Bridal Veil Falls by tiny Luna Island. Both falls are about 176 feet (54 m) tall. And together, they measure 1,060 feet (323 m) wide.

Canadian Falls is located between Goat Island and Queen Victoria Park. It is the largest part of Niagara Falls. This waterfall is about 167 feet (51 m) tall and 2,600 feet (792 m) wide.

Niagara Falls Area

American Falls

Bridal Veil Falls

Luna Island

Goat Island

Prospect Point Park

Queen Victoria Park

Canadian Falls

Thousands of years ago, North America was covered by ice. This time was called the Ice Age. When the ice melted, water flooded the land.

The flooded areas formed the Great Lakes and the Niagara River. Over time, the powerful, moving water **eroded** the land. This created Niagara Falls.

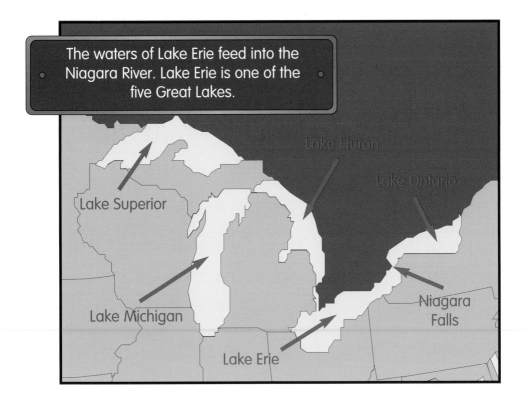

The waters of Lake Erie feed into the Niagara River. Lake Erie is one of the five Great Lakes.

Lake Huron

Lake Ontario

Lake Superior

Lake Michigan

Lake Erie

Niagara Falls

Today, the Niagara River's rushing water continues this **erosion**. The land changes very slowly as water falls over the cliffs of Niagara Falls.

Powerful Waters

Water flows fast over Niagara Falls. Every second, more than 600,000 gallons (2.3 million L) of water rush over the falls! The falls are an important source of **hydroelectric** power. They provide energy for people in Canada and the United States.

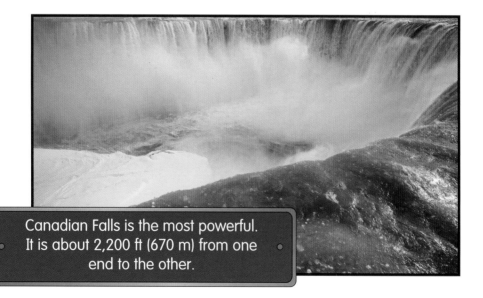

Canadian Falls is the most powerful. It is about 2,200 ft (670 m) from one end to the other.

During the summer months, water flow is usually greater during the day. This makes the falls fuller and more impressive to visitors.

The amount of water flowing over Niagara Falls changes throughout the year. Hydroelectric **power plants divert** some of the water into special **reservoirs** before it reaches the falls. There, a system of pipes turns the water's movement into energy.

In the past, people have become famous by going over the falls and surviving.

In 1829, Sam Patch jumped from a tower into the falls. In 1859, Jean Francois "Blondin" Gravelet crossed over the falls on a tightrope.

In 1876, Maria Spelterina crossed Niagara Falls by tightrope several times. She was just 23 years old!

In 1901, a 63-year-old teacher named Annie Edson Taylor rode over the falls inside a barrel. She was the first person to do this.

Other people have attempted similar acts through the years. But, such activities are very dangerous. They are also against the law.

Annie Edson Taylor was strapped down inside the barrel for safety.

In 1911, Bobby Leach went over Canadian Falls. He built two other barrels before he decided to use a steel one.

Millions of people have visited Niagara Falls. Today, this is still a popular area.

It is possible to visit both the U.S. and Canadian sides. People can see American and Bridal Veil falls from Prospect Point Park in New York. And, people can view American and Canadian falls from Queen Victoria Park in Canada.

At the parks, people can hike and tour the falls. And, they can take boat rides on *Maid of the Mist*.

People can ride near the falls aboard *Maid of the Mist*. Boats have been bringing tourists to the falls since 1846.

Detour ⬇

Did You Know?

. . . There are two different cities named Niagara Falls. One is in New York and the other is in Ontario, Canada.

. . . On July 9, 1960, seven-year-old Roger Woodward fell into the Niagara River. He went over the Canadian Falls wearing only a life preserver! The *Maid of the Mist* boat rescued him at the bottom of the falls.

. . . For a short time on March 29, 1848, Niagara Falls stopped completely! Some people thought the water froze. But, the real cause was an ice jam in the Niagara River.

Most winters, the falls only partially freeze. But during the ice jam of 1848, people were able to walk out onto the riverbed!

Niagara Falls Today

Today, people continue to visit Niagara Falls throughout the year. It is a popular vacation spot.

Niagara Falls also remains an important natural **resource**. Its powerful waters provide energy to homes and businesses.

Some people are worried Niagara Falls may become **overdeveloped**.

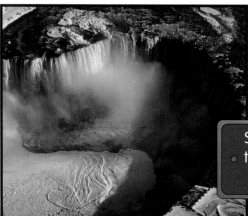

So, they are working to preserve it for the future.

Scientists say that Niagara Falls continues to change. Thousands of years from now, it may not even exist anymore.

Important Words

divert to turn away from.

erode to wear away.

hydroelectric a type of power that is produced by using flowing water.

landmark a feature that is easily recognized.

overdevelop to grow or refine too much.

power plant a place with machinery and structures used to create energy.

reservoir a pool or a tank used for holding liquid.

resource something that is useful.

WEB SITES

To learn more about Niagara Falls, visit ABDO Publishing Company on the World Wide Web. Web sites about Niagara Falls are featured on our Book Links page. These links are routinely monitored and updated to provide the most current information available.
www.abdopublishing.com

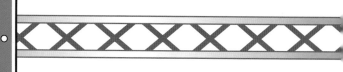